SIMPLY CHUBBY
A
CELEBRATION OF LIFE

BY DOCIA SMITH
ILLUSTRATED BY: DERRICK LEE MITCHELL

First Printing, Asta Publications, LLC, trade paperback edition, December 2011
ISBN:978-1-934947-56-2
LCCN: 2011960911

No part of this publication may be reproduced, stored in a retrieval system, or transmitted in any form or by any means, electronic, mechanical, photocopying, recording, or otherwise, without written permission of the publisher.

A percentage of the proceeds will go to the P.E.A C. E Foundation. The Protecting Endangered At-Risk Children Everywhere was created to educate and protect children.

For information regarding permission, write to:
Asta Publications,
Permissions
P.O. Box 1735
Stockbridge, GA 30281

Text and Illustrations Copyright by Docia Smith
Illustrated by Derrick Lee Mitchell

All Rights Reserved

Printed in the U.S.A.

SIMPLY CHUBBY

A

CELEBRATION OF LIFE

CHUBBY

I dedicate this book to all the parents, grandparents, sisters, brothers, uncles, aunts, and friends who have lost a child at the hands of someone who should have loved and cared for them.

This book is a "Celebration of Life", although a short one on this earth...yet powerful among those who are left behind to remember and never forget their presence.

I was born to my Mommy Erica, my big brother DaMir and a host of other people who loved me.

Later I found my Daddy Dennis who fell in love
with me and all of my ways.

Daddy and I had so much fun when we were together. He played ball with me and he took me to fun places like Chucky Cheese.

My favorite things to do was to play with my brother and sing Patty Cake.

I loved eating all kinds of food.

That is how I got my nickname Chubby.

I loved all the hugs and kisses I could get from people.

My mommy especially loved kissing my face.

I loved eating with anyone who would let me.

Everyone who loved me always wanted to be in my pictures. Of course, I did take one or two by myself.

I loved people and people loved me.

I had lots of friends at my daycare.

I loved playing with the blocks, building them up only to knock them back down.

There are many things I will never do because I am not here anymore, but there are so many things I did do in my short time here.

I laughed, I played, I smiled at you, I gave you hugs, I touched your face, and I touched your heart.

Most of all I loved you and you loved me!

Now I live in a place where peace, joy laughter, and love rules.

Chubby

The day I heard we (I) lost you at the hands of someone near...
Sadness filled my heart
Anger filled my thoughts
Today my heart is filled with the joy of knowing you,
The anger is no longer in my thoughts
Because I choose to think of your smile that brightens up any room
That you graced your presence with.

Grandma Docia

To God Be The Glory

I am Docia Smith born in Memphis, Tennessee and raised in Ohio. Widow, mother of Toshia, Dennis, DeAonte and DeMario, grandmother to Micha, Miya, DaMir, and Anthony (deceased).

Graduate of East Technical High, earned Associates Degree in Early Childhood and now seeking a B.A. in Early Childhood Education.

This is my first of many children's books with the help of my Father from above, and Chubby who inspired me to tell his story.

I choose to celebrate his life and to remember all the wonderful things about him.

Special Thanks to my son, Dennis.